# STRUCTURAL REFORM OF THE FEDERAL BUDGET PROCESS

William A. Niskanen

American Enterprise Institute for Public Policy Research
Washington, D. C.

William Niskanen is professor of economics in the Graduate School of Public Policy, University of California at Berkeley.

Domestic Affairs Study No. 12, April 1973

ISBN 0-8447-3099-8

Library of Congress Catalog Card No. L.C. 73-79384



*Printed in United States of America*

# STRUCTURAL REFORM OF THE FEDERAL BUDGET PROCESS

# CONTENTS

# PREFACE

The first draft of this study was completed during the summer of 1972, in the interim between my former position as assistant director for evaluation of the Office of Management and Budget and my new position as a professor at the Graduate School of Public Policy at Berkeley. Since completing that draft, two events have had an important bearing on the issues addressed in this study:

First, federal spending and taxation were major issues of the 1972 presidential campaign. The Nixon administration made a commitment to constrain the growth of federal spending and a somewhat conditional commitment not to increase federal taxes. The reelection of the President by a large margin suggests broad public support for this position.

Second, Congress seriously addressed and later rejected the President's request for discretionary authority to reduce spending in order to hold fiscal 1973 outlays within a $250 billion ceiling. One outcome of this unusual episode was a new congressional Joint Study Committee on Budget Control. This committee provides the appropriate forum to review the fiscal policy instruments described in Chapter 1 of this study.

The published version of this study includes no changes to reflect the issues of the 1972 presidential campaign or the results of the election. The study concludes, for example, that an increase in tax rates may be an important part of a strategy to constrain the growth of federal spending. On the other hand, the first draft was changed to reflect the congressional debate on setting an effective spending ceiling and the establishment of the new joint study committee.

Several changes in the text have also been made as a consequence of the comments and constructive criticism of Sam Cohn, Larry Korb, Dan Larkins, Phil Marcus, David and Attiat Ott, Rudy Penner, Steven Rhoads, Murray Weidenbaum, and Aaron Wildavsky. My friendly critics do not share all the views expressed in this study, so I must bear the responsibility for any errors and unsupported assertions.

# SUMMARY

This study addresses four major flaws in the federal budget process that have contributed to the growing perception that the federal budget is "out of control." For each flaw, a specific reform is suggested, one that, in general, would be consistent with the incentives of the major participants in the federal budget process and would not require a reform of our fundamental political institutions. These four flaws do not cause all of the many problems presented by the federal budget process, but resolution of the larger set of problems probably would require some changes in our political institutions.

1. At the present time, there is no explicit nexus between aggregate federal spending and tax rates. As a consequence, both major functions of fiscal policy—the efficient allocation of the nation's resources between the federal and nonfederal sectors and the stabilization of the national economy at low rates of unemployment and inflation—are undermined. Chapter 1 suggests a new "marginal balanced budget policy" that would establish a dollar-for-dollar relation between marginal federal spending and expected tax revenues around an outlay target approved by Congress. It also outlines several changes in the congressional budget process designed to implement this policy.

2. The annual value of a large amount of resources used by the federal government (roughly $30 billion a year) is not included in the total federal budget or in the budgets of the agencies using these resources. As a result, most of these unbudgeted resources are overused, and the accounting of both the total resource cost of the federal government and the relative resource cost of major federal activities is incomplete. Chapter 2 suggests modifications in the executive budget process intended to force agencies to recognize the total annual

cost of their activities and to permit them to change the combination of budgeted and unbudgeted resources.

3. Most federal budget decisions are made without effective consideration of the future costs of present decisions. As a consequence, in some instances decisions are made to commit the federal government to large future spending and to forego opportunities to reduce future spending that would have been made differently with appropriate accounting and balancing of present and future costs. Chapter 3 suggests several changes in the executive budget process that would improve the incentives of both agencies and the budget director to balance present and future costs more efficiently.

4. The executive budget process operates without effective prior policy guidance. This results in inadequate staff work on most major issues, redundant staff work on other issues, and a general failure to consider policy and budget issues beyond the current budget cycle. Chapter 4 outlines a policy planning and review process within the executive office designed to improve policy guidance both for the agencies and in the subsequent executive budget review.

Any decision process, including the federal budget process, should be evaluated by the quality of its decisions, not by the apparent simplicity and rationality of the process. Those who are satisfied with the outcomes of the present federal budget process have no reason to be concerned about that process, however complex and irrational it may appear to be. Those who are concerned about the outcomes, however, should focus their attention on improving the process rather than on merely decrying the outcomes. For those who share this concern, this study suggests the general characteristics of selected reforms that deserve serious discussion and, possibly, the test of experience.

# INTRODUCTION

## The Basis for Concern

A consensus is developing that the federal budget is "out of control." This concern is expressed by the public and by officials in both the administration and Congress.[1] It is manifest in increasing pressures for tax reform, as well as for structural reform of the congressional budget process. The objective basis for this concern is less clear, but probably includes at least the following conditions:

- Although Nixon's first budget message proposed a balanced federal budget, the four budgets from fiscal 1971 through 1974 indicate a cumulative deficit of around $100 billion.
- Since 1965, federal spending has increased at a substantially faster rate than the increase in national output.
- Around two-thirds of present federal spending is "uncontrollable" without a change of legislation.
- For the first time in American history, total federal spending did not decline with a major reduction in war spending.
- Also, for the first time, there is no prospect in the five-year budget planning horizon for a balanced federal budget, even at full

---

[1] In October 1972, Congress considered and finally rejected a proposal for a $250 billion outlay ceiling for fiscal 1973 involving a temporary grant of discretionary authority to the President to reduce any federal program to maintain the ceiling. Although the Senate rejected this measure, the fact that it was proposed by the Ways and Means Committee and approved by the House suggests a general concern that the present budget processes are considered inadequate to constrain total federal spending.

employment, unless present programs are reduced or tax rates increased.[2]

Any one or more of these conditions, of course, may have been generally desired and is not sufficient evidence that the budget is out of control. Also, any narrowly based concern about the results of the budget process may only reflect the view of a small group that would prefer more special benefits and/or lower taxes. A general concern about the results of the budget process, however, is a manifestation, not that the budget cannot be controlled, but that the budget process is not coherent—that is, that the aggregate of decisions on the budget components is not consistent with the desired budget totals. It is important to recognize that the federal budget is the result of a collective choice process, and not of an inexorable process such as the progression of the planets or radioactive decay. Thus the budget's forecasts of spending and revenues are estimates of the results of a decision process, and that process itself reflects decisions made over many years. The federal budget and the federal budget process, given time and energy, can be anything that we collectively want them to be.

## The Traditional Approach to Budgetary Reform

The traditional approach to federal budgetary reform dates from the Commission on Economy and Efficiency appointed by President Taft in 1911.[3] This commission proposed a comprehensive executive budget to include both expenditures and revenues, based on both existing legislation and new legislation proposed by the President. The commission also proposed a detailed classification of expenditures by function and by current expenses versus capital outlays—in addition to the traditional classifications by object class and organization. Interestingly, the early support for federal budgetary reform resulted from a recognition that the congressional budget system did not provide sufficient control of federal spending, which was then around $2 billion a year. For most of American history to that time, the primary fiscal problem of the federal government had been that the

[2] The fiscal 1973 budget documents provide adequate documentation of the present and recent fiscal conditions. For an interesting forecast of fiscal conditions in the near future see David Ott et al., *Nixon, McGovern, and the Federal Budget* (Washington, D. C.: American Enterprise Institute, 1972).

[3] Arthur Smithies, *The Budgetary Process in the United States* (New York: McGraw-Hill Book Co., 1955), provides an effective summary of the history of this commission and of subsequent budget reform measures.

federal revenue system (based on customs duties, alcoholic beverage taxes, and land sales) generated substantially more revenue than Congress believed appropriate to spend! A decade later, after a major change in fiscal conditions, the primary recommendations of this commission were incorporated in the Budget and Accounting Act of 1921, which authorized a comprehensive executive budget, the creation of the Bureau of the Budget, and the creation of the General Accounting Office. Congress expected that a presidential budget review would provide the necessary discipline for "economy and efficiency" in federal spending.

Most of the budget reforms that have been proposed and approved since that time build on the primary recommendations of the Taft Commission—to make the federal budget more comprehensive, to strengthen presidential budget review, and to provide more detailed information on federal spending. The Corporation Control Act of 1945 required an annual presidential review of the total expenditures of wholly owned government corporations. The Legislative Reorganization Act of 1946 provided for legislative budget review and approval of total spending. The Budget and Accounting Procedures Act of 1950 required a functional presentation of federal expenditures. The General Appropriation Act of 1950 affirmed the power of the Bureau of the Budget to apportion the rate of obligations against appropriations to avoid deficiencies and unnecessary expenditures. (This apportionment power is a form of item veto that has been a point of intermittent controversy between the President and Congress.) The shift of focus from the administrative budget to the consolidated cash budget in fiscal 1964 and adoption of the unified budget in fiscal 1969 further broadened the range of activities included within the presidential budget review. The executive branch experiment with the formal Planning, Programming, and Budgeting (PPB) System—with its focus on functional (program) accounts and five-year spending estimates—led Congress, in the Legislative Reorganization Act of 1970, to require submission of similar information in the budget documents.

The traditional budget reform movement appears to have run its course. Most of the recommendations of the major budget commissions and studies have been adopted and some, such as the legislative budget and the formal PPB system, have been abandoned. Two recent suggestions for reform of the federal budget process represent rather minor modifications of earlier proposals: The Brookings analysis of the fiscal 1973 budget concludes with a proposal for three-year authorizations and appropriations, primarily to permit more intensive (but less frequent) review of major programs.[4] The AEI analysis of the fiscal 1973 budget suggests adding reviews of "artificially uncontrollable" programs and of credit programs to the annual budget review process.[5] These recent proposals have obvious merit, but they are most unlikely to resolve the major problems leading to the currently perceived federal budget crisis.

## The Structural Approach to Budgetary Reform

Any current analysis of the federal budget process must start by resolving a dilemma: Over the past half-century, most of the recommendations derived from the traditional approach to budget reform have been adopted but, nonetheless, the federal budget seems to be increasingly "out of control." A recognition that most of the traditional budget reforms have been designed to provide more *information* to the decision makers helps resolve this dilemma. The usually implicit assumption of these reforms is that decision makers desire and can absorb the additional information and that the incentives and constraints on the decision makers are such that additional information will improve the quality of their decisions. At the present time, however, additional information does not appear to be important to the quality of federal budget decisions. A case could be made that officials in the presidential and congressional budget review process acquire, with some effort, all the information they desire and can effectively use, subject to the general inability to predict the future and the general recognition that government agencies are not expected to incriminate themselves. Those public officials most concerned about a specific program are seldom surprised by additional information on the costs and effects of that program. As the preparation and absorption of additional information is itself costly, any person or institution operates in a state of rational ignorance. The outcomes of a budget process operating with full information will differ in only minor ways from the outcomes of the present process, unless the additional information somehow affects the incentives and constraints of the critical budget decision makers.

One example of a budget reform originally defended as providing better information that significantly changed the constraints on budget decision makers was the development of progressively more

[4] Charles L. Schultze and others, *Setting National Priorities: The 1973 Budget* (Washington, D. C.: The Brookings Institution, 1972), pp. 464-68.

[5] Murray L. Weidenbaum and Dan Larkins, *The Federal Budget for 1973* (Washington, D. C.: The American Enterprise Institute, 1972), pp. 53-55.

comprehensive federal budgets. The basic aim of the budget director is to hold "the" proposed budget to the desired fiscal target. The more comprehensive the budget subject to review and public attention, the easier it is to achieve the desired fiscal target. As a consequence, not surprisingly, the major changes leading to a more comprehensive budget have originated in the executive branch. Although these changes have been represented as generally beneficial procedural changes, they have had significant effects on the fundamental political decisions with respect to the level and composition of federal spending and revenues.

The most important change in the comprehensiveness of the federal budget was the shift of focus from the traditional administrative budget to the consolidated cash budget (including trust fund spending and revenues). This purportedly neutral change in budget concepts has had an impact on programs and possibly also on total spending trends. First, it gave the budget director an incentive to constrain trust fund spending and to support increases in trust fund revenues in order to "borrow" the trust fund surplus to finance other programs. Thus, the change in part accounts for the slow growth of federal highway spending and the rapid growth of social security taxes since 1964. Advocates of those programs for which spending has been constrained have reacted in a predictable manner: the Export-Import Bank was removed from the budget in 1971 and the social security system was changed to a current financing basis in 1972. Second, since the consolidated cash budget usually has a larger surplus or a lower deficit than the administrative budget, the change may have contributed to the rapid growth of total federal spending since that time.

The subsequent changes in federal budget concepts had smaller, but still interesting, effects. For fiscal 1968 only, the President's budget proposal focused attention on the national income accounts (NIA) budget, possibly because the expected deficit was much smaller in that budget than in the consolidated cash budget. In fiscal 1969, the budget proposal emphasized the unified budget, which differs only nominally from the consolidated cash budget, and all subsequent budgets have been presented on this basis. The unified budget provides the budget director with several types of opportunities for meeting the fiscal target that are not available under the national income basis. For example, whereas the NIA budget does not include proposed asset sales, the unified budget reports them as negative outlays. Also, whereas the NIA budget is estimated on a delivery and accrual basis, the unified budget is estimated on a cash payments and receipts basis. These opportunities have led budget directors to propose substantial and increasing asset sales (that have not been fully realized) and to shift payments between adjacent fiscal years in order to achieve their fiscal targets. These two types of activities induced by the unified budget concept lead to misrepresentation of the total cost of the proposed federal programs in a given year.

The main point of the above examples, of course, is that changes in budget concepts and procedures should not be evaluated in terms of *instrumental* criteria—such as comprehensiveness, detail, procedural rationality, control, et cetera. Rather they should be evaluated in terms of the *outcomes* of the budget process. If changes in the budget process do not lead to different budget outcomes, they are redundant. If process changes do lead to different budget outcomes, the probable effects of these process changes should be recognized and evaluated by the political system with which this nation makes such decisions. One should not expect the political system to approve knowingly changes in the budget processes that threaten the fundamental distribution of political power. If politically feasible changes in the budget processes do not lead to satisfactory budget outcomes, the only recourse is to change the political system.[6]

The structural approach to budgetary reform has three distinguishing characteristics: it focuses on the incentives and constraints of the key budget decision makers; it provides an explicit statement of the probable effects of changes in the budget process on budget outcomes; and it also provides an explicit statement of the value premises of the suggested budgetary reforms.

This study discusses reforms in the federal budget process that would be compatible with the present political system. It does not consider changes in the way federal officials are elected or in congressional voting rules. The specific convictions of the author are that the federal budget is too large, is growing too fast, includes too many programs that yield benefits only to small regions and sectors of the national economy, and uses too much of certain types of resources. Those who do not share these convictions have reason to be satisfied with the present budget process. The selected structural reforms of the budget process outlined in this study are offered in the belief that there exists a sufficient consensus on these problems for these reforms to deserve serious consideration.

---

[6] The best general statement of this position is by Aaron Wildavsky, "Political Implications of Budgetary Reform," *Public Administration Review*, vol. 21 (Autumn 1961), pp. 183-90.

# 1
# FISCAL POLICY

## The Problem

Fiscal policy is the set of rules determining total government spending and revenues. For many years, total federal spending was held to a level roughly equal to the tax revenues expected during that period. And state and local governments generally set spending for current operations and interest payments to equal current revenues, using bond issues to finance major capital projects. Such traditional fiscal rules characteristically establish some relation between government spending and revenues and serve primarily to allocate resources between the government and other sectors of the economy.

In recent decades, however, a case has been made that the federal budget should be set to stabilize the national economy at low rates of unemployment and inflation. The Kennedy and Johnson administrations endorsed this general fiscal policy but made no commitment to a specific rule for determining the budget totals. The first three Nixon budgets endorsed three different fiscal rules: The proposed fiscal 1971 budget embraced the traditional balanced budget rule—that total federal spending should be roughly equal to the tax revenues expected in that year. The proposed fiscal 1972 budget, coming after a year of unsatisfactory performance of the national economy, endorsed the rule that total federal spending should be no more than the tax revenues that would be generated that year if the national economy were operating at full employment.[1] The proposed fiscal 1973 budget endorsed the slightly modified rule that full

[1] This rule was originally proposed by the Committee for Economic Development in 1947. See "Taxes and the Budget: A Program for Stability in a Free Economy," Committee for Economic Development, 1947.

employment *spending* (total spending less the incremental spending for unemployment compensation and public service employment at the actual higher employment rate) should be no more than full employment revenues. Each successive change in the fiscal rule permitted higher spending and a larger deficit than did the preceding rule. Although recent administrations of both parties have endorsed the general fiscal policy of the "new economics," no administration has yet been prepared to commit itself to a specific fiscal rule for an extended period. (Indeed, one cannot reread the presidential budget and economic messages of the last decade without suspecting that expressed fiscal policy has been as much a rationalization of the results of the executive budget process as an effective constraint on these results.)

Federal fiscal policy is now charged with two major functions—first, efficient allocation of the nation's resources between the federal and nonfederal sectors and, second, stabilization of the national economy at low rates of unemployment and inflation. This study makes no evaluation about the general merits of such a fiscal policy. Rather it argues that, at best, the present federal budget process can perform one or the other of these functions, but not both. The evidence of the last several years suggests that the increasing focus placed on the stabilization function has undermined the allocation function without making an effective contribution to stabilizing the economy. The primary reason for both of these effects is that the *marginal* dollar of federal spending is financed, partly or wholly, by increasing the federal deficit. An understanding of these two effects requires some explanation.

The allocation function is best served when the marginal dollar of federal spending is financed wholly from taxes. Federal deficits do not appear to exert as strong a constraining influence on expenditures as do current taxes, in terms of either the incentives of federal officials or the perception of the public. This is true with respect to the spending decisions of federal officials for several reasons: Changes in the deficit can be attributed to prior decisions, or to current decisions made by other parts of the government. Moreover, the "new economics" provides a rationale for explaining federal deficits as a means for stabilizing the economy but does not provide an accepted rule for determining the optimal deficit. Both the President and Congress appear to be more willing to permit an increase in the deficit, which may be rationalized either as out of their control or as desirable under current economic conditions, than to approve a tax increase. For its part, the public does not appear to perceive the cost of federal spending financed by a deficit to be as high as the cost of spending financed by current taxes for several reasons: If the deficit is financed by borrowing from the public, the cost is both deferred and diffused in ways that are not widely understood—primarily through the lower economic growth attributable to the displacement of private investment. If the deficit is financed by money creation, the cost is diffused in the form of inflation that the public often attributes to other causes.[2] (The federal government, of course, has an obvious incentive to contribute to this illusion and has a rather consistent record of blaming other causes for a deficit-fed inflation.)

According to the above argument, the total level of government output and spending demanded will be higher if tax rates are set to generate an expected deficit than if the rates are set to generate a budget balance or surplus. One should expect, therefore, a positive relation between the rate of increase in federal spending and the proportionate size of the deficit (relative to federal spending)—that is, total federal spending should grow most rapidly during periods of expected deficit. An expected deficit, by understating the perceived cost of federal programs, creates an "excess demand" for federal output and spending which, in turn, increases the deficit. (For given tax rates and national income, of course, an increased deficit is an *arithmetic* consequence of additional spending; but there is no necessary reason for this positive relation because, over some interval, both spending and tax rates are subject to political control.) For several interesting conditions, the excess federal spending, beyond that which would be desired if tax rates were set to achieve an expected balance, is roughly equal to the size of the actual deficit, and the value of this excess spending may be as low as one-half this amount.[3]

---

[2] For completeness, it should be recognized that federal deficits do not always displace private investment or cause inflation. For the general conditions prevailing since World War II, however, deficits should be expected to induce one or the other of the above effects.

[3] This conclusion is not obvious, and the analysis here is a bit complex. Start with the traditional assumption that the equilibrium level of government services is where the marginal value of these services to the median voter is equal to his (perceived) share of the marginal cost of these services. Add the assumptions that his actual share of the cost of government services financed by a deficit is the same as his share of total taxes but that his perceived share of the cost of a deficit is lower than his actual share. For these conditions, the excess amount of this median voter's share of government spending is equal to his actual share of the deficit. In the limit, if the median voter perceives that his share of the costs of spending financed by a deficit is zero, government spending will be increased to a level where the marginal value of government services to this voter is zero, and the value to him of the additional services financed by a

**Table 1**

CHANGES IN NATIONAL OUTPUT, FEDERAL SPENDING, AND THE DEBT

| | Average Annual Rate of Change in: | | |
|---|---|---|---|
| **Period** | Net national product | Federal expenditures | Gross federal debt |
| 1869-1873 to 1912-1916 | 4.1% | 2.1% | −1.5% |
| 1920 to 1929 | 1.5 | −8.0 | −4.4 |
| 1929 to 1939 | −1.3 | 13.1 | 11.3 |
| 1946 to 1965 | 6.2 | 6.8 | 1.1 |
| 1965 to 1972 | 7.7 | 10.4 | 4.9 |

**Notes:** All rates of change in current dollars (not corrected for inflation). Federal expenditures on Treasury basis through 1929, national income accounts basis since 1929.

Gross federal debt on Treasury basis. For 1946-1965 period, federal deficit reduced slightly on national income accounts basis.

Both earlier and recent American experience demonstrates a general relation between the rate of increase in federal spending and the proportionate size of the federal deficit (see Table 1).[4] For most of American history through the 1920s, federal spending ranged between 1 and 3 percent of national output, with most of the variation attributable to spending for current and prior wars. For almost all the peacetime years in that period, the federal budget was in surplus. Federal spending increased to 11 percent of net national product in 1939 and to 42 percent in 1945, during a period when there were large proportionate deficits in every year. Over the 20-year period from 1946 through 1965, total federal spending increased only slightly faster than net national product, and the federal budget had a surplus in roughly half of these years and a small cumulative

deficit will be around one-half his actual share of the deficit. The problems of aggregation from the median voter to the total federal budget necessarily make any normative conclusions about the total budget much more tentative.

4 A more accurate test of the hypothesis that deficit financing induces a rapid increase in federal spending, of course, should isolate the obvious short-run effect of increased government spending, for given tax rates and national income, on the size of the deficit. Over the long periods described in this paragraph, however, tax rates were also changed, and there is no obvious reason for any long-run effect of government spending on the frequency and proportionate size of the deficit.

surplus over the period. Following the 1964 tax reduction, federal spending increased at a rapid rate, again in association with large sustained deficits. Total federal spending increased from around 20 percent of net national product in 1965 to around 24 percent in 1972; the federal budget had a surplus in only one of these years and a large cumulative deficit over the period.[5]

Some of those who are concerned about the growth in federal spending argue that the best way to retard this growth is to reduce taxes. The argument and evidence summarized above suggest that a tax reduction would *strengthen* the demand for additional federal spending. Federal spending appears to increase at roughly the same rate as national output when the federal budget is maintained in approximate balance. Federal spending appears to increase most rapidly when incremental spending is financed by deficits, and the rate of increase appears to be positively related to the proportionate size of the deficit. After a period of sustained deficits, a tax *increase* may be necessary to reduce the excess demand for federal spending.

A fiscal policy that, in practice, generates an open-ended deficit in most years clearly undermines the allocation function. A dominant concern for the allocation function provides the traditional basis for the balanced budget rule—a rule which effectively constrains federal spending by keeping it within expected tax revenues. A balanced budget rule, however, is not the only rule that would induce a more efficient allocation between the federal government and the rest of the economy. The only necessary fiscal condition is that the *marginal* spending dollar is a tax dollar, and, as demonstrated later, this condition can be consistent with any amount of planned fiscal stimulus or restraint. Although, in practice, the increasing concern for the stabilization function has undermined the allocation function of fiscal policy, there does not appear to be any necessary reason for this conflict of objectives. The major current challenge of fiscal policy is to develop and implement procedures that can contribute to both the allocation and stabilization objectives.

A second major result of financing marginal federal spending partly or wholly by increasing the deficit is that the amount of fiscal stimulus or restraint cannot itself be controlled with any precision. The presidential budget review is the only part of the federal budget process where joint consideration of total spending, total revenues, and fiscal policy occurs. The record of the period since World War II, however, indicates only a weak relation between the amount of fiscal

[5] Both the fiscal and national output data on which these observations are based are measured on a calendar year, national income accounts basis.

stimulus proposed in the President's budget and that finally realized. In part, this is due to conditions that were not anticipated during the presidential budget review. In part, it reflects the fact that the President's budget is not an unbiased estimate of projected spending and revenues. And, in part, it is a result of the phenomenon discussed above—namely, that fiscal policy itself affects the demand for federal programs and spending, and this secondary effect is not incorporated in the original estimates.

The post-World War II record of the relation between the planned amount of fiscal stimulus (or restraint) and the amount realized is summarized in Table 2 and is discussed below.[6]

1. For the period from fiscal 1947 through fiscal 1972, the actual annual change in total federal expenditures in the national income

**Table 2**

RELATION OF ACTUAL AND PROPOSED FISCAL VARIABLES, 1947-1972

| | $\hat{\alpha}$ | $\hat{\beta}$ | $R^2$ |
|---|---|---|---|
| Federal expenditures | .038<br>(3.2) | .953<br>(13.2) | .879 |
| Federal revenues | .062<br>(3.2) | .071<br>(.3) | .005 |
| Federal deficit | .022<br>(.7) | −.189<br>(.5) | .009 |

**Notes:** For federal expenditures and revenues, the regression form was the following:

$$[\log_e A_t - \log_e A_{t-1}] = \alpha + \beta [\log_e P_t - \log_e E_{t-1}] + u_t$$

where

$A_t \equiv$ actual level on national income accounts
$P_t \equiv$ proposed level in President's budget
$E_{t-1} \equiv$ estimated level for prior year in President's budget

For federal deficit, the regression form was the following:

$$\frac{AD_t}{AX_t} = \alpha + \beta \left(\frac{PD_t}{PX_t}\right) + u_t$$

where

$AD_t \equiv$ actual deficit on national income accounts
$AX_t \equiv$ actual expenditures on national income accounts
$PD_t \equiv$ proposed deficit in president's budget
$PX_t \equiv$ proposed expenditures in President's budget

Numbers in parentheses are "t" statistics.

[6] These conclusions are based on statistical analysis by the author. Bob Berry assisted me in this analysis. Details available on request.

accounts (the variable most generally used to represent the gross expenditure stimulus) was nearly 4 percent per year *plus* the percent increase in the President's proposed budget. Over 80 percent of the variance in the actual percent change is related to the percent change in the proposed budget. For the decade beginning in fiscal 1963 (the first budget prepared by the Kennedy administration), this same relation holds. However, less than 50 percent of the variance in the actual percent change in expenditures during this period is related to the percent change in the proposed budget. This suggests that the executive branch has a moderate ability to control the rate of increase in total federal spending, although the actual percent increase is generally higher than that proposed and the controllability of the actual increases appears to have deteriorated during the period when the fiscal policy of the "new economics" has been formally endorsed.

2. From fiscal 1947 through fiscal 1972, the actual percent change in total federal receipts in the national income accounts was over 6 percent per year. This change is unrelated to the forecasted percent increase in the President's proposed budget, suggesting that the executive branch has had little ability either to control or forecast the rate of increase of federal revenues.[7] In other words, there is no information content in the forecast of total federal revenues presented in the President's budget, given the level of revenues in the prior year.

3. For the entire post-World War II period, the actual federal surplus or deficit in the national income accounts (expressed as a percent of total expenditures in each year) has been *unrelated* to the surplus or deficit forecasted in the President's budget. This suggests that the executive branch has also had little ability either to control or forecast the *net* fiscal restraint or stimulus of the federal budget. Again, this indicates that there is no information content in the estimated federal surplus or deficit presented in the President's budget, in spite of (or, more likely because of) the extraordinary distortion of the budget process to achieve a specific proposed amount and the presumed political sensitivity of this figure.

All in all, the ability of the executive branch to control or forecast the primary fiscal variables is unimpressive. Although the federal budget may serve an automatic stabilizing function, the information or the instruments for pursuing a discretionary fiscal policy do not appear in hand. This general problem is not specific to the United States. Other national governments, most importantly the United

[7] To be fair to the revenue estimators, these forecasts are based on existing or proposed tax rates that may later be changed and on forecasts of economic conditions that are subject to considerable error.

Kingdom, that have tried to change their budgets to improve specific temporal conditions in the economy have had similar difficulty in producing the desired amounts of fiscal stimulus or restraint.[8]

The above record suggests a moderate relation between the gross expenditure stimulus proposed in the President's budget and the amount realized, but no relation between the proposed and actual net fiscal stimulus. In addition, it should be recognized that there is considerable controversy about the effects on the national economy of the *actual* amounts of fiscal stimulus, given the level of the aggregate money supply. The sectarian controversy among economists concerning the relative effects of fiscal and monetary variables will not be resolved soon and are not central to this study. Whatever the effects of the actual amount of fiscal stimulus, however, fiscal policy cannot be an effective discretionary stabilization instrument unless the amount of fiscal stimulus can be more effectively controlled. The federal budget process does not appear to have performed either the allocation or the stabilization function of fiscal policy well.

## A Suggested Structural Reform

One way to resolve the dilemma posed by the two functions of fiscal policy would be to direct fiscal policy solely to one or the other. The case for limiting fiscal policy to the allocation function is that the federal budget is a crude and/or ineffective instrument for stabilizing the economy, that the money supply can and should be used as the primary stabilization instrument, and that the traditional balanced budget rule has proved quite effective in restraining the rate of increase in federal spending. However, most of the public now expects the government to use the budget to stabilize the national economy. The contrary case for focusing fiscal policy on the stabilization function is that the money supply is a crude and/or ineffective instrument for stabilizing the economy and that some other instruments of the federal budget process can and should be used to perform the allocation function. The main problem with this approach is that no other instrument—such as the presumed constitutional limits on federal functions, outlay and debt ceilings, or more flexible use of the apportionment powers, et cetera—has been effective in holding back the demand for federal spending financed by an increased deficit.

[8] For an interesting summary of the British experience, see Aaron Wildavsky, *Community and Policy* (tentative title) (London: Macmillan, forthcoming).

The public clearly expects the federal government to perform both of these functions, whether through fiscal policy or in some other manner. And fortunately one need not choose between them. The two major problems discussed above both spring from one condition—namely that the *marginal* dollar of federal spending is financed, partly or wholly, by increasing the deficit. The elimination of this one condition is necessary to resolve both problems. The one essential characteristic of a fiscal policy capable of performing both the allocation and stabilization functions is that, after some desired amount of fiscal stimulus or restraint, any increase (or decrease) in federal spending be wholly financed by increasing (or decreasing) some broadly based and broadly perceived tax. This form of fiscal policy is best described as a "marginal balanced budget policy." Under it, the total federal budget could have whatever planned surplus or deficit was believed appropriate given expected economic conditions,[9] but any approved *change* in federal spending above or below the level consistent with the desired fiscal effects would be balanced by an approved change in tax rates to generate an equal change in expected tax revenues.

The general characteristics of a process designed to implement a "marginal balanced budget policy" are summarized below.[10]

1. The first stage of the budget process under the proposed approach would not differ from present practices. The process would start with the submission of the President's budget, usually late in January. This budget would propose a total spending level, estimate the revenues expected from the current tax system and any proposed changes, estimate the expected economic conditions, and discuss the appropriate fiscal policy for these conditions.

2. Soon after Congress received the proposed budget, some joint or select committee consisting of the leadership of the major fiscal committees would conduct a formal fiscal policy review. Using data submitted by the administration, its own staff, and outside sources, this committee would review the proposed spending and revenue totals, the expected economic conditions, and the proposed fiscal policy. It would then submit a resolution establishing an outlay *target* for the next fiscal year for all activities included in the unified budget, and this resolution would be subject to approval by both

---

[9] A convincing analysis of the considerations that determine the optimal amount of surplus or deficit at full employment is presented in Martin Bailey, "The Optimal Full-Employment Surplus," *Journal of Political Economy*, vol. 80, no. 4, pp. 649-61.

[10] The general characteristics of this process were suggested to me by Peter Fox in November 1970.

houses and the President. This part of the process would be similar to the ill-fated "legislative budget" process established by the Legislative Reorganization Act of 1946, with two critical exceptions: (1) the outlay constraint would be a *target,* not a ceiling, and (2) most important, the resolution could provide for an automatic change in the personal income tax to generate revenues equal to the *difference* between total approved outlays and targeted outlays, given the expected economic conditions.[11]

3. After approval of the resolution establishing the outlay target and the tax trigger, Congress would review each spending bill "on its own merit," as it does now.[12] If the total outlays approved by Congress, including those for programs not requiring annual appropriations, exceeded the approved outlay target by some threshold amount, personal income tax rates would automatically be increased (without any additional legislation required) to generate expected revenues equal to the outlay difference. Conversely, of course, if the total outlays approved by Congress were less than the threshold, personal income tax rates would be automatically cut to reduce expected revenues by the outlay difference.

The new approach is designed primarily to establish a dollar-for-dollar relation between *marginal* federal spending (relative to the outlay target) and expected personal income tax revenues. This condition, as explained above, should improve the execution of both the allocation and the stabilization functions of fiscal policy. Changes in the personal income tax would make the public face up to the current tax cost of marginal federal spending, and every congressman contributing to a spending decision would be forced to defend the tax effects of the aggregate of these decisions. The process would contribute to the stabilization function because it would control the expected surplus or deficit in absolute amounts. If actual economic conditions should differ from those expected at the time the outlay target was set, the actual surplus or deficit would also differ from that expected in a countercyclical direction. This process, thus, would hold the expected surplus or deficit to that planned in setting the

[11] Several people have suggested that the automatic tax trigger should be broadened to include both the personal and the corporate income tax. This may have more political appeal, but the uncertainty about the incidence of the corporate income tax might weaken the effect of the tax change on the popular demand for federal spending.

[12] Congress may find it valuable to use a "scorecard" system, such as that proposed by Murray Weidenbaum, to relate individual spending decisions to the desired outlay target. See Murray L. Weidenbaum and John S. Saloma, *Congress and the Federal Budget* (Washington, D. C.: American Enterprise Institute, 1965), pp. 76-81.

outlay target and still permit countercyclical variations in the actual deficit to reflect current economic conditions.

Several lesser effects of this general process should also be recognized. Given the expected revenues, Congress would be formally approving a target surplus or deficit when it established an outlay target. The behavior of Congress with respect to reviewing and approving debt increases suggests that its members would be most unlikely to give formal approval to as large a target deficit as the deficit they would allow to develop informally (which can always be attributed to decisions by other congressmen or to the administration). The probable effect of a formal review and vote on a target deficit would be to set a more constraining target outlay and target deficit than would be likely to result under the present process. Recognition of this effect may undercut the proposal's support among those who favor increased government spending and have the opposite impact on those who favor less government spending. One other lesser effect of the proposed process would be to accelerate congressional review and approval of appropriation bills, a period that now extends well into the new fiscal year. In a fiscal year for which the outlay target was expected to be "tight" (and most years would probably be tight unless Congress were willing to approve a large target deficit), every committee addressing a spending decision would have a strong incentive to keep its bill from being the one that would have to be substantially reduced if it were not to trigger a tax increase. Recognition of this effect might lead those subcommittees that traditionally consider their bills late in the review period to resist the proposal, but the significant problems typically created by late appropriations would probably cause the administration to support it.

The general outlines of the process described above must be fleshed out with considerable institutional detail before adequate evaluation is possible. This detail is important to both its approval and effectiveness, because the process necessarily involves the distribution of power within the government. The special issues that must be resolved and the proposed resolutions of these issues are discussed below. The list is probably not exhaustive, and the resolutions are only illustrative and tentative, pending more careful review by the administration and Congress.

**1. Composition of the review committee.** The most direct historical precedent for a fiscal policy review committee was the Joint Committee on the Legislative Budget established by the Legislative Reorganization Act of 1946. This committee included all the members of the appropriations and finance committees of both houses or a duly authorized subcommittee. It had no separate staff. There is a general consensus that the committee was too large to be effective and that it should have had a small permanent professional staff.

The perceived inadequacies of this committee led to several different proposals for establishing congressional review of total federal spending and revenues. In 1952, Senator John McClellan introduced a bill to create a Joint Committee on the Budget consisting of seven members from each of the two appropriations committees supported by a permanent joint staff; the bill was passed by the Senate in 1952 and in numerous subsequent years, but has never been approved by the House. In 1955, Arthur Smithies proposed a Joint Budget Policy Committee of 18 members—the chairmen and ranking minority members of the two appropriations committees and the two finance committees, four members from the Joint Economic Committee, and six members from Congress at large.[13] In 1965, John Saloma proposed a Joint Committee on Fiscal Policy of, at most, 20 members drawn primarily from the two appropriations committees and the two finance committees.[14]

The common characteristics of these three proposals—including, most importantly, the fact that no one was approved—may provide some guidance in formulating a new proposal. First, reflecting the unfortunate experience with the legislative budget, the proposed committees would have only a review and advisory role. The primary problem in making the idea of a legislative budget work was that Congress was unwilling to operate within a rigid spending ceiling. Initially, it was reluctant to fit specific appropriations within a rigid ceiling and, later, it was not prepared to set a ceiling without knowing the sum of the specific appropriations. The committee that formulated the legislative budget scheme had been aware of the problem of fitting parts within a whole and it had proposed that, if the sum of appropriations exceeded the approved total, each appropriation would be automatically reduced by the same proportion in order to stay within the ceiling. This idea, which would have created a perverse incentive to pad each appropriation bill, was fortunately not included in the Legislative Reorganization Act of 1946, but unfortunately the final bill included no provision for resolving this problem. These three proposals, while avoiding the problems of a rigid budget total, did not advocate committees with substantive responsibility. Congress, probably appropriately, has decided that the establishment of

[13] Smithies, *The Budgetary Process in the United States*, pp. 192-97.

[14] Weidenbaum and Saloma, *Congress and the Federal Budget*, pp. 181-83.

yet another group to review and advise its membership on the budget is worth neither the effort nor the risk of creating false expectation that more information, by itself, will have a significant impact on budget outcomes.

Second, each of these proposals would have created a *joint* committee. Most members of Congress, however, have opposed the creation of permanent joint committees for any other than very specialized issues. A select committee on fiscal policy in each house appears to be more acceptable to Congress, even if it uses a common staff.

The desirable characteristics of a fiscal policy review committee (or committees) appear to be that the committee should be small, it should include the ranking members of the major fiscal committees, it should have the services of a permanent professional staff, and a select committee in each house is probably preferable to a joint committee.

The most important of these characteristics is that the joint or select fiscal policy committee should include the ranking majority and minority members of the major fiscal committees. My suggestion is that a House Select Committee on Fiscal Policy, for example, include the two ranking majority members and the ranking minority member from both the Appropriations Committee and the Ways and Means Committee, and the one ranking member of both parties on the Joint Economic Committee; this select committee, thus, would have five majority members and three minority members drawn from three regular committees. The chairmanship of this committee would rotate annually between the chairman of the Appropriations Committee and the chairman of the Ways and Means Committee. A similar select committee would be established in the Senate. The question of whether these two select committees should have separate staffs or a common staff does not appear to be crucial. It is important, however, that the staff have a reputation for objectivity and professionalism similar to that of the staff of the Joint Committee on Internal Revenue Taxation.

**2. Scheduling of fiscal policy review.** The competing pressures on the scheduling of fiscal policy review are (1) to provide sufficient time for an effective review and (2) to arrive at an approved outlay target prior to the reporting out of any spending bill. The Legislative Reorganization Act of 1946 required that the legislative budget be reported by February 15. However, it was soon recognized that this date, which was only a few weeks after receipt of the President's budget, did not allow sufficient time for an effective fiscal policy review. In 1949, the due date for the legislative budget was postponed to May 1. In that year, most of the appropriations bills had already been passed by that time, but in more recent sessions of Congress, only a few appropriations bills have been reported this early. The two dates of February 15 and May 1 probably bracket the desirable deadline for approval of an outlay target. A twofold requirement that the outlay target be approved by April 1, or by the time the first spending bill is reported, is suggested. This would typically provide around ten weeks for congressional fiscal policy review after receipt of the President's budget and would not significantly constrain the review of spending legislation.

**3. Estimates of outlays.** The President's budget is presented in terms of both requested budget authority and estimated outlays deriving from this budget authority. The presidential fiscal policy review and the estimated surplus or deficit are based on estimated outlays. The congressional appropriation review, however, focuses on budget authority, and appropriations bills formally approve budget authority without directly affecting outlays in a specific fiscal year. A congressional fiscal policy review should also be based on outlays, as this measure of the estimated rate of spending more closely approximates the financing requirements and economic impact of federal activities than does budget authority. In order for an outlay target to constrain spending decisions effectively, outlay estimates for each spending bill must be made as the bill is being reviewed. The institutional questions involved are these: Who is to make the outlay estimates? How are any differences in specific outlay estimates, say, between those made by the administration and those made by Congress, to be resolved, if at all?

At the present time, the federal agencies and the Office of Management and Budget are best prepared to make the outlay estimates, because these estimates require a detailed knowledge of the operation of individual programs and the estimation procedures are somewhat arcane. Congress is probably unwilling to rely solely on administration estimates, however, on the ground that this would give the administration undue influence over individual program decisions. As a minimum, it appears, Congress should establish an outlay estimating staff similar to the staff of the Joint Committee on Internal Revenue Taxation that now estimates the revenue yields of tax legislation. This may be the best argument for a permanent joint staff supporting the select committees on fiscal policy, although the estimation function could also be performed by the staffs of the appropriations committees.

Some rule also must be established to resolve any difference in the outlay estimates between those prepared by the administration and those prepared by Congress. One such rule would be to use a simple average of the competing estimates. Another rule, possibly preferable because it would have a more constraining effect on spending decisions, would be to use the higher of the two estimates. Generally, the people making estimates of a particular phenomenon constitute a rather close community, and the history of the relations between the Treasury Department and the Joint Committee on Internal Revenue Taxation suggests that substantial differences in the estimates prepared by separate groups are seldom likely to develop—even though all of the estimates may be quite inaccurate. The outlay estimation problem would probably provide the basis for some maneuvering between competing groups but is unlikely to undermine the effectiveness of the general process.

**4. Form of the tax change.** The effectiveness of this proposal would be dependent on changes in a broadly based and broadly perceived tax. For this reason, the automatic tax changes should probably be restricted to the personal income tax.[15] The primary question is whether the tax change should be an equal change in the marginal rates across the income tax schedule or an equal percent surcharge. At present, a one percentage point increase in all marginal income tax rates would yield additional revenues of around $5 billion and would increase tax payments per taxpayer in proportion to his taxable income. A 5 percent personal income tax surcharge would yield about the same amount but would increase tax payments per taxpayer in proportion to his present tax payments. As the present personal income tax is now somewhat progressive relative to income, an equal percentage point increase in marginal rates would make the tax structure more nearly proportional, and an equal percent surcharge would maintain the general progressivity of the present tax structure. The choice between these two forms of tax change, of course, depends on one's judgment about who should pay how much taxes. This choice would not affect the general effectiveness of this proposed process but may affect its acceptability.

**5. Outlay threshold for the tax change.** For administrative convenience and popular impact, the automatic tax changes should probably be restricted to discrete intervals, say, a one percentage point change

---

[15] Again, a case has been made to apply the tax trigger to both the personal and corporate income tax, so this issue also should be addressed.

in marginal tax rates or a 5 percent surcharge. In this case, no purpose is served by triggering a discrete tax increase if the estimated total outlays are only nominally above or below the approved outlay target. In addition, outlay estimates are not precise and a precise stabilization of the planned fiscal effects is unnecessary. One suggested procedure would be to set the tax trigger at 1 percent of the approved outlay target for the initial tax change and at 2 percent for subsequent changes. If the outlay target were $250 billion, for example, taxes would not be changed if the total estimated outlays were within $2.5 billion (plus or minus) of this target. A difference between the outlay target and total approved outlays of $2.5 to $7.5 billion would trigger a $5 billion revenue increase, a difference of $7.5 to $12.5 billion would trigger a $10 billion revenue increase, and so forth. The incentive for fiscal constraint would be highest in the intervals adjacent to the outlay target. In the example used here, the approval of estimated outlays $2.5 billion above the target would trigger a $5 billion tax increase and, conversely, the approval of estimated outlays $2.5 billion below the target would trigger a $5 billion tax reduction. Although total outlays cannot be estimated within 2 percent with high confidence, the use of larger intervals would undermine the fiscal discipline of this process.

6. **Timing of the tax change.** When should the automatic tax changes become effective? The appropriate timing of the tax change is complicated by the noncoincidence of the fiscal year and the tax year and by the extended review of spending bills, amendments, and supplementals throughout the fiscal year. The allocation function would be best served if the tax changes were announced prior to November, at least in election years. The stabilization function would be best served if the timing of the change in tax payments approximated the timing of the change in government spending. All of these issues cannot be resolved by any single timing rule.

One suggested rule would be to change personal income tax liability and withholding rates effective January 1, based on all spending actions through November plus the estimated outlays for spending bills in the President's budget that were not approved by that time. This would allow one month for estimating the total approved outlays, for reconciling any differences in estimates, and for calculating and announcing the automatic tax changes. This rule would have the advantage of changing tax rates only at the beginning of the tax year. If changes in federal spending should be delayed by late approval of the spending bills, the rule also would provide for a near coincidence of the change in spending and tax payments.

Early approval of the appropriations bills, however, would cause the change of tax payments to lag the change in federal spending by up to six months. This rule would provide an undesirable incentive to delay approval of any appropriations bill larger than that recommended by the President until after November, in order to avoid triggering a tax increase. Also the public would not be informed about the tax changes until after the general elections.

Another rule deserving consideration would be to change personal income tax liabilities and withholding rates effective the beginning of the second month following approval of all regular appropriations bills. Like the first rule, this one would also allow at least a month for determining and announcing the tax changes. But there are several noteworthy differences. This rule would have the disadvantage of changing tax rates during the tax year, requiring a prorating of the change over the year. On the other hand, it would usually reduce the lag between the change in federal spending and the change in tax payments, particularly when the regular appropriations bills were approved early in the fiscal year. Moreover, it also would have the advantage of basing the automatic tax changes on all regular appropriations bills (and any amendments and supplementals approved prior to approval of the last regular bill). But this rule still would provide an incentive to add supplementals late in the year to avoid triggering a tax increase. Since this rule would provide for a variable timing of the tax change, Congress should be expected to accelerate appropriation actions that, in total, would trigger a tax reduction prior to the general elections and, conversely, to delay actions that would trigger a tax increase.

The short-run effectiveness of this general process—in serving both the allocation and stabilization function of fiscal policy—is quite dependent on the timing of the automatic tax changes, so these and other timing rules deserve serious consideration.[16]

### Summary Comments

Both the administration and Congress contribute to the problems of implementing an effective fiscal policy. Although the administration has assumed the primary role in formulating fiscal policy, no administration to date has developed successful procedures to serve both the allocation and stabilization functions of fiscal policy. The inter-

[16] Some consideration should also be given to a rule that any nonappropriation bill that changes federal spending (such as revenue sharing and social security payments) be effective no sooner than the beginning of the next fiscal year.

mittent presidential request for discretionary spending and taxing authority reflects concern about this failure, but Congress has been understandably unwilling to grant this authority. Congress's one major experiment with formulating and implementing a legislative budget was a dramatic failure. The major reform in the federal budget process suggested in this chapter requires the understanding and approval of Congress. In contrast with the proposals for presidential spending or taxing authority, the proposal would affirm the primary authority of Congress to formulate and implement fiscal policy. At the same time, it would broaden the policy role of Congress, because the procedure would ensure that Congress share with the administration the responsibility for formulating the appropriate fiscal policy each year, and it would facilitate implementation of that fiscal policy by establishing appropriate constraints on the aggregate spending decisions of Congress. There is ample evidence of widespread support within Congress for the objectives of a legislative budget but, as yet, there is no consensus on an acceptable procedure. The reform described here is put forth in the belief that Congress wants to exercise a greater responsibility for fiscal policy and would be willing to adopt a procedure that would make its own spending decisions more consistent with the desired fiscal policy.

It is also important to recognize that the suggested reform is consistent with any desired fiscal policy, whether a slow or rapid increase in federal spending or a surplus or deficit of any size is believed desirable. The proposal is designed to increase the effectiveness of whatever fiscal policy Congress endorses by constraining both total federal spending and the expected net fiscal stimulus or restraint to the levels formally approved by Congress.

Some skepticism has been registered concerning the willingness and ability of Congress to assume a primary role in establishing fiscal policy and to develop a coherent federal budget. Such skepticism is consistent with the recent House approval of temporary authority for the President to reduce spending for any federal program. This unusual action can also be interpreted as reflecting a general sense of crisis about the federal fiscal condition. In any case, the final rejection of this authority and the establishment of the new Joint Study Committee on Budget Control suggests a willingness by Congress both to accept a primary responsibility for fiscal policy and to consider new instruments to implement this policy. The suggested reform described in this chapter may prove to be the appropriate instrument.

# 2
# UNBUDGETED COSTS

## The Problem

The federal budget is a proposed plan of cash payments and receipts. It does not correspond with any conventional business account, and neither a balance sheet nor income statement for the total federal government is prepared. The federal budget, unfortunately, does not accurately reflect the relative or total annual cost of resources used by federal activities, measured in terms of their values in other uses. Outlays by many agencies and for the federal government as a whole are substantially lower than the annual cost of federal activities, because the annual costs of some resources acquired, held, and used by federal agencies are not fully reflected in their annual budgets. For example, outlays by the Atomic Energy Commission, one agency that maintains "businesslike" accounts, are around 80 percent of the total annual cost of AEC activities. The information necessary to make this calculation is not available for most agencies. For some resources, agency budgets include no costs and for other resources, outlays are less than their annual value in other uses. The probable consequences of a failure to include the full annual costs of these resources in agency budgets include: (1) overuse of these resources, relative to other inputs to the same activity, (2) overexpansion of the activities using these resources, relative to other activities, and (3) overexpansion of the federal government, relative to the rest of the economy.

In most cases, agencies do not know the total annual cost of their activities, and they have no incentive to develop such information. The mere availability of such information, however, would be insufficient to resolve the allocation problems resulting from the failure to include some costs in the budget. The necessary conditions for efficient behavior by federal agencies are that they must have to defend the *total* annual cost of their activities and they must be permitted to reallocate spending between budgeted and unbudgeted resources. Again, as the history of the traditional budget reform movement demonstrates, an increase in the information about federal activities is unlikely to change the outcomes of the budget process, unless it is combined with a change in the incentives and constraints of those responsible for budget decisions.

The major resources for which the budget understates annual costs and a *very rough* estimate of the annual costs not included in the budgets of the using agencies are summarized in Table 3. The remainder of this chapter discusses the institutional conditions specific to each of these resources and the basis for the estimates of unbudgeted costs.

**1. Land and structures.** The federal government owns over 750 million acres, around one-third of the total U.S. land area. In addition, it now owns around 2.5 billion square feet of building space and a large number of specialized structures and facilities (airfields, ports, roads, dams, et cetera). In general, this real estate is "free" to federal agencies. Most of the land has been public domain since it was first incorporated within the United States. The total cost of acquired land,

**Table 3**

MAJOR UNBUDGETED COSTS

| Major Underbudgeted Resources | Net Annual Unbudgeted Costs (estimated) |
|---|---|
| Land and Structures | $21 billion |
| Manpower | |
| Underfunded civilian pensions<br>Unfunded military pensions<br>Veterans benefits<br>Conscription | $ 6 billion |
| Nuclear Materials, Weapons, Reactors | |
| Annual acquisitions<br>Present stock | $ 3 billion |
| Nonmarketed Resources | |
| Electronic frequency spectrum<br>Airspace and control services | ? |

buildings, and structures is included in the federal budget in the year of purchase, but sometimes not in the budget of the using agency. Most importantly, federal agencies pay no current "rent" on federally owned real estate.

As the annual rent on this real estate is not included in the agency budgets, the use of these resources is not subject to periodic review, either within the agency or by the presidential and congressional budget review processes. Agencies have no incentive to release real estate for other uses unless the budget outlays associated with the use of the property are higher than its annual value. Transfers of real estate within the government involve no financial exchange, and any revenues from sale or outlease accrue to the Treasury. In addition, transfers within the government are restricted by the right of first refusal by each successive organizational level, and transfers to nonfederal users usually require special legislation. As a rule, agencies have an incentive to overuse real property, to neglect developments that would improve the value of property in other uses, and to resist property disposal. Other agencies and nonfederal organizations that may want to acquire some federal real property are often deterred by the extraordinarily complex system for property transfer.[1]

A comprehensive, detailed assessment of federal real property has not been made, and no office has yet been charged with this responsibility. The government property records report the cost of property in the year of acquisition, but most of this information has little value in developing estimates of current property values. A 1971 study prepared for the Property Review Board, fortunately provides the basis for making a rough estimate of the current total value of federal real property.[2] This study developed estimates of (1) the average value per acre of urban and rural land by type of use and (2) the average value per square foot of building space by use from the purchase costs of all such land and buildings acquired by federal civilian agencies in the 1966-1970 period. These average values can then be multiplied by the total physical inventory by use to provide an estimate of the total value by use and a grand total of land and buildings. For the period in question, the estimated average value was around $10,000 per acre for urban land, around $100 per acre for rural land, and around $24 per square foot of building space. This

[1] Jora Minasian, "Land Utilization for Defense," in Stephen Enke, ed., *Defense Management* (Englewood Cliffs, New Jersey: Prentice Hall, 1967), pp. 232-45, summarizes the major problems of federal agency land use.

[2] Report of the Ad Hoc Inventory Task Group to the Property Review Board, May 1971.

gross assessment procedure cannot be applied to the heterogeneous category of other structures and facilities, so such property was valued at its original cost. The resulting estimates of the total value of federal real property are summarized in Table 4.

These estimates are based on a number of heroic assumptions and must be considered very rough. Moreover the procedure probably underestimates the total current value of federal real property. Since 1968, the midpoint of the period from which the average value estimates were prepared, the general price index has increased around 20 percent and the price index on nonresidential structures has increased around 40 percent. The current replacement cost of the other structures and facilities is surely higher than the original cost and the value is probably also higher, although much of it has limited alternative use and is overbuilt. (In addition, these estimates do not include the value of any mineral rights, either underground or offshore.) A somewhat arbitrary increase of 20 percent in the total value of land and a 40 percent increase in the total value of buildings and other structures and facilities yields an estimate of the total value of federal real property of around $240 billion in 1972 dollars. The total annual value of federal real property is estimated at 10 percent of the estimated total value of land (to reflect the average real pretax return on private investment) and at 12 percent of the estimated total value of buildings, structures and other facilities (to reflect the real pretax return on private investment plus depreciation). This yields a total annual "rent" on federal real property of nearly $27 billion. It is interesting to note that this unbudgeted rent is around 25 percent of total federal purchases of other goods and services.

This procedure provides a credible estimate of the total annual value of federal real property, but any institution developed to charge

**Table 4**

ESTIMATED VALUE OF FEDERAL REAL PROPERTY, 1968

(in billions)

| | Civilian | Military | Total |
|---|---|---|---|
| Urban land | $ 1.8 | $13.8 | $ 15.6 |
| Rural land | 69.3 | 2.1 | 71.3 |
| Buildings | 15.8 | 44.0 | 59.8 |
| Other structures and facilities | 22.3 | 14.9 | 37.2 |
| TOTAL | $109.1 | $74.8 | $183.9 |

rent on individual units of property must develop a much more refined assessment procedure. From this total, current outlays of around $5.5 billion for direct federal construction should be subtracted to yield a net unbudgeted annual cost of federal real property of around $21 billion.

**2. Manpower.** Manpower outlays in federal agency budgets do not accurately reflect the total annual cost of current manpower for the following primary reasons:

- The Civil Service pension fund is underfunded: the combined government and employee contributions to the fund are lower than the amount necessary to finance the expected future pension benefits.
- The military pension system is completely unfunded: the Department of Defense budget includes the current outlays to retired military personnel (outlays that are attributable to manpower used in prior years) but does not include the increase in pension liabilities for current personnel.
- Expectation of future veterans benefits probably permits the military to acquire manpower at lower current defense outlays. (If veterans benefits do not reduce current military manpower costs, these benefits are a pure windfall to veterans, however deserved.)
- As of fiscal 1973, military salaries and benefits for some positions were still insufficient to fill present force levels without conscription.

The general effect of these conditions is that the agency budgets understate the total annual cost of current federal employees. It is not clear that this causes a general overuse of manpower, because the total annual cost of major types of capital assets is also understated, but it surely causes an overuse of those types of manpower for which the budget outlays are relatively low.

Only very rough estimates of the difference between the total annual cost of current manpower and the budgeted outlays for manpower can be made without further study, but these estimates are sufficient to illustrate the general magnitude of the unbudgeted costs. Current annual funding of the civil service pension fund is around $4 billion, including employee "contributions" of $2 billion and an equal amount from the employing agencies. This current funding would be roughly equal to the increase in pension liabilities only if there were to be no further increase in civil service salaries. As civil service pension benefits are based on the high three-years' salary prior to retirement, however, any increase in civil service salaries increases the pension liabilities by more than current funding. A

1967 study by the Cabinet Committee on Federal Staff Retirement Systems estimated that current funding of civil service pensions would have to increase by around 50 percent to provide full funding of pension benefits, based on a 4¾ percent annual increase in civil service salaries.[3] (The actual increase in civil service salary scales has been significantly higher than this rate in recent years.) For fiscal 1973, a 50 percent increase in current funding would amount to around $2 billion; the actual increase in unfunded pension liabilities is probably somewhat higher because of the large increase in civil service salaries. This $2 billion of unfunded pension liabilities is around 7 percent of the total budgeted manpower costs for civil service personnel.

Current annual outlays for retired military personnel are $4.3 billion, and this cost of prior military service is included in the Department of Defense (DOD) budget. But the annual increase in the pension liabilities due to currently employed military personnel is not included in the defense budget. Several years ago, the Department of Defense actuary estimated the annual increase in military pension liabilities at around $3.5 billion, and the current increase is probably higher because of the large recent increases in military salaries. Thus the budgets of the several military services understate the total annual cost of currently employed military personnel by, at least, the amount of the annual increase in unfunded military pension liabilities, probably around $4 billion. This amount is about 18 percent of the budgeted cost of military personnel. On the other hand, the total Department of Defense budget may overstate the total annual cost of current military personnel: Payments to retired personnel are larger than the estimated increase in military pension liabilities, and this difference will increase substantially over the next decade with a near doubling of the annual payments to retired personnel. The DOD manpower budget, thus, will become an increasingly inaccurate estimate of the annual cost of current military forces.

The differences between the total annual cost of military manpower and the budgeted outlays that are attributable to expectation of future veterans benefits and to conscription cannot be estimated from published budget data. The budget of the Veterans Administration, now around $12 billion a year, is not a useful basis for estimating how much the DOD budget would have to be increased if *prospective* veterans benefits were reduced. Any estimate of the

---

[3] *Federal Staff Retirement Systems*, Senate Document No. 14, 90th Congress, 1st Session, 1967, pp. 250-51.

relation between current military salaries and expected future veterans benefits would have to be developed by statistical techniques, and no such estimate has been made. The amount by which defense manpower outlays would have to increase if prospective veterans benefits (other than medical care and compensation for service-connected disability) were eliminated is probably small because potential military enlistees lack knowledge of current veterans benefits, are uncertain about future benefits, and discount future benefits at a high rate. But this statement cannot be made with high confidence prior to statistical test or actual change in prospective veterans benefits. Conscription has recently been ended. Fiscal 1973 military manpower outlays would probably have had to be up to $1 billion higher if conscription had been terminated one year earlier, but the fiscal 1974 budget is based on voluntary enlistments.

Including only the unfunded civil service pension liabilities of around $2 billion and the unfunded military pension liabilities of around $4 billion, the total amount by which annual manpower costs exceed budgeted outlays for current personnel is estimated to be around $6 billion. This total underfunding of manpower costs would be higher by the amount by which expected future veterans benefits reduce current military manpower outlays and if conscription is reinstituted.

**3. Nuclear materials, weapons, and reactors.** The Atomic Energy Commission produces nuclear materials; it develops, tests, and produces nuclear weapons; and it develops and produces nuclear reactors for use by the Department of Defense. Outlays for these activities are included in the AEC budget, not in the Department of Defense budget. It is the AEC that directly defends the proposed budget for these activities in the presidential and congressional budget review. The Department of Defense establishes the "requirements" for the output of these activities but does not defend the cost of these requirements and does not have the opportunity to reallocate spending between the military activities funded in the DOD budget and those funded in the AEC budget. The exclusion of defense-related AEC activities from the defense budget induces the AEC to supply all that is required and the Department of Defense to require all that can be supplied, regardless of the value of these resources or the production assets in other uses. The potential allocation problems of this condition are substantially moderated by the presidential and congressional budget review, but these reviews are necessarily captive of the information provided by the supplying and using agencies.

In addition, the present stock of nuclear weapons includes a large amount of nuclear materials produced in prior years. This material has a substantial value in other uses, either as reactor fuel or in new weapons. The Department of Defense now pays no "rent" on the annual value of these materials, and this part of the annual cost of defense is not included in any part of the federal budget. DOD has an incentive to hoard nuclear materials as long as their value in present use is higher than the small budget outlays for management and storage. The presidential and congressional budget review has been relatively unsuccessful in reducing this allocation problem.

The President's budget provides sufficient information for a moderately precise estimate of the annual cost of new materials, weapons, and services provided by the AEC to the Department of Defense. The proposed fiscal 1973 budget provides the following figures:[4]

| *AEC Budget Totals* | *$ in Millions* |
|---|---|
| Total budgeted costs | $2,362.7 |
| Plus: Total nonbudgeted costs | 634.2 |
| Total annual costs | $2,996.9 |
| Total budgeted direct costs | $2,189.4 |
| Estimated "overhead" rate | 36.8% |

The total annual cost of new materials and services supplied to DOD is estimated as follows:

| *AEC Activity* | *Direct Budgeted Cost* + | *"Over-head"* = | *Annual Cost* |
|---|---|---|---|
| Nuclear materials | $ 426.6 million | 36.8% | $ 583.6 million |
| Less: Nonfederal income | | | 263.5 |
| Defense materials | | | 320.1 |
| Weapons | 877.7 | " | 1,200.7 |
| Space power | 35.0 | " | 47.9 |
| Naval reactors | 149.8 | " | 204.9 |
| Total | | | $1,773.6 |

[4] *The Budget of the United States Government 1973 Appendix* (Washington: U.S. Government Printing Office, 1972), pp. 771-77.

A disproportionate amount of the nonbudgeted costs and some part of the other direct costs (for example, general reactor technology, nuclear safety, physical research, et cetera) are probably also attributable to defense uses, so the above estimate is probably slightly low. The above procedure attributes the indirect and nonbudgeted costs in proportion to the direct budgeted cost of the defense-related AEC activities. Although this is somewhat arbitrary, the annual cost of new nuclear materials and services supplied to the Department of Defense must be close to $1.8 billion.

Any estimate of the annual cost of nuclear materials in the present weapons inventory, even one developed from classified information, is necessarily subject to large error and is strongly dependent on the rate at which the nonmilitary uranium inventory is disposed. The published budgets, however, provide the basis for a very rough estimate: since the establishment of the AEC, a cumulative total of around $12 billion of nuclear materials has been produced, valued at original direct production cost and net of nonfederal revenues from nuclear materials and enrichment services. This is a very rough estimate of the current capital value of the military stock of nuclear materials—because real production costs have declined over this period, the general price level has increased, and some of the nuclear materials produced are held in a nonweapons inventory. As the physical depreciation on most of this material is negligible, the annual value of this material is estimated to be 10 percent of this very rough estimate of the capital value, or around $1.2 billion. This estimate represents only the general magnitude of the annual value of these materials and must be refined prior to establishing any system for charging the military for these materials. The total annual cost of nuclear materials, weapons and reactors used by the military, thus, is probably around $3 billion, and the potential allocation problem resulting from excluding this annual cost from the defense budget should be evaluated relative to this estimate.

**4. Nonmarketed resources.** The federal government uses several important resources for which market prices are not established either within the government or in the private sector. The most important nonmarketed resources used by the government are (1) the electromagnetic frequency spectrum and (2) the airspace and air traffic control services. The proportionate use of these resources by the federal government can only be estimated in physical terms, as no estimate of the value of these resources has been made.

The federal government, primarily the military, uses around 20 percent of the frequency spectrum between 25 and 5,000 megaHertz and shares another 30 percent or so of this most valuable part of the spectrum. This allocation has been remarkably stable since World War II.[5] Within the government, frequency allocations are made by the Interdepartment Radio Advisory Committee reporting to the Office of Telecommunications Policy. Most such allocations, in effect, are based on historical use but some reallocations are made based on expressed statements of "need" and the available spectrum space. Spectrum-using agencies are not now charged any fee for this resource and they have an obvious incentive to overuse the spectrum and to hoard spectrum rights for possible future use. The Office of Telecommunications Policy is now considering several types of mechanisms for basing spectrum allocations on the value of spectrum rights, either by using the estimated values as additional information affecting the centralized reallocation decisions or by establishing a system of formal direct charges on spectrum rights and permitting voluntary transfers within the government. This complex problem is not likely to be resolved soon, but current efforts within the federal government are far ahead of any efforts to rationalize the allocation of spectrum rights among nonfederal users.

The federal government, again primarily the military, uses a significant proportion of the nation's airspace and air traffic control services, also without any payment by the using agencies. Around 22 percent of the controlled en route flight events and around 6 percent of the terminal events are attributable to government airplanes. The en route airspace is seldom congested, and, although the major terminal areas are often congested, government airplanes usually use separate terminals with different approach and departure corridors, so the value of the airspace used by government airplanes is probably negligible. On the other hand, air traffic control services involve annual federal outlays of around $1.2 billion a year. Around 17 percent of these outlays, or around $200 million a year, appear to be attributable (on an average cost basis) to government use. These costs are included in the FAA budget but not in the budgets of using agencies. On net, the government use of the airspace and air traffic control services does not appear to represent a sufficient cost to merit a different allocation mechanism, at least until the airspace becomes more congested and/or air traffic control services become more costly.

[5] Harvey Levin, *The Invisible Resource* (Baltimore, Md.: The Johns Hopkins Press, 1971), p. 50.

## A Suggested Structural Reform

Agency budgets do not reflect the total annual costs of the above resources for different reasons: some resources, such as conscripted manpower, are acquired by the government at less than full value. Some resources, such as nuclear materials and some land and structures, are acquired by the government at full value but are transferred between agencies at less than full value. Some resources, such as career military and civil service manpower, are acquired at a current cost less than full value by promising future pension benefits that are not fully funded in current budgets. Finally, for some resources, such as the frequency spectrum and the airspace, no private market exists, and the government has allocated these resources among agencies without any payment to reflect their value in other uses.

The underbudgeting of those resources creates allocation problems. Although the detailed institutional approaches for resolving these problems are likely to differ, they must have two characteristics in common. First, agencies must be forced to defend the total annual cost of the resources they use, at least in the presidential budget review. Second, agencies must have the opportunity to reallocate spending between the budgeted and unbudgeted resources—subject, of course, to presidential and congressional review.

The primary issue affecting the selection of a process for each of these resources is whether to change the scope of agency budgets for the presidential review only or for both the presidential and congressional review. At this stage, given the very rough estimates of the unbudgeted costs and a poor understanding of the best procedures for budgeting these resources, it is probably appropriate to restrict any changes in the scope of agency budgets to those presented and defended in the presidential budget review, at least for an experimental period. And a change of the "internal" agency budgets may be sufficient if better allocation decisions on an internal total annual cost budget reduce the total net outlays on the "external" cash payments budget.

The problem of gaining approval for any reform is to convince those whose approval is necessary that the reform serves their interests. The primary problem in gaining approval of total annual cost agency budgets is that no public official has much direct interest in the efficient use of resources. Agency managers generally act to increase their command over resources. The presidential budget director is most strongly motivated to report a proposed federal budget that is within the fiscal target, given the accepted budget concept for the external budget. Agencies that use a large amount of underbudgeted resources are likely to oppose any reform that would increase the budget cost of these resources. Other agencies and nonfederal groups may favor such a reform, because it would increase their potential command over these resources; but, out of lack of experience, they are unlikely to realize the full value of using these resources. The critical official who must be convinced of the value of reform is the director of the federal Office of Management and Budget. A change in the accepted budget concept to include the total annual cost of federal activities would have the desired effect, but this would also require the understanding and acceptance of Congress, and this does not appear feasible in the near future. A second approach is to demonstrate that an internal review of a total annual cost budget is likely to reduce the net outlays on the current unified budget concept, either by reducing outlays for the budgeted resources or by increasing offsetting receipts by the sale or outlease of the underbudgeted resources. At the present time, it appears, the case for internal total annual cost budgets must be based on a demonstration of this effect.

The general characteristics of a reform to move toward total annual cost budgeting for each of these resources are summarized in the following paragraphs. The procedures suggested are only illustrative and do not exhaust the alternatives that should be considered. A substantial effort would be necessary to develop the appropriate procedures for each resource, and the objective of this section is to make the case for undertaking this extended task.

**1. Land and structures.** One step that would substantially improve the review of land and structures costs would be to implement a general policy of leasing, rather than purchasing, all acquisitions of land and general purpose structures. The advantages of a general leasing policy are the following: the total annual cost of using newly acquired real property would be included in agency budgets in each year of use, rather than only at the time of purchase; this would induce a periodic review of the use of this real estate by both the agency and in the presidential budget review process. The real property would be retained on the local property tax base, thus avoiding a reduction of local tax revenues or an increase in federal impacted aid. Budget outlays in the acquisition year would be lower, thus making it easier for both the agency and the budget director to finance capital improvements within a tight budget. And last, in general, the government is prepared to lease buildings that do not meet the unnecessarily restrictive building specifications that are applied to purchased buildings. In addition to the value of facilitating annual budgeting of real property costs, a leasing policy should enable the government to acquire buildings at a total discounted cost equal to or lower than the cost of purchase, except in the rare case when the government may be subject to a monopoly lease bid. The Public Buildings Amendments of 1972 broadened the authority of the executive branch to lease real property, and a consistent application of a recent Office of Management and Budget circular would lead to more general use of leasing. Congress, however, has usually opposed the leasing of buildings for government use, and the implementation of a general leasing policy would require its understanding and approval.

For real property now owned by the government and any additional property that would be purchased, some form of rental charge system would be necessary to ensure that the annual cost of this property would be included in agency budgets and subject to periodic review by the agency and the presidential budget reviews. The several institutional problems that must be addressed are the following:

- What types of real property should be subject to annual rents and to possible transfer or disposal?
- On what basis should the annual rents be established?
- What organization(s) should be responsible for assessing the real property and establishing the annual rents?
- How should the annual rents be incorporated in the agency budgets for the agency and presidential budget reviews?

A rental charge system with the following general characteristics is suggested as a tentative response to the above questions:

Only that real property with a substantial value in alternative uses should be included in the rental charge system. No purpose is served by charging rents on property whose value is specific to its present use, whatever this value. It would probably be appropriate to exclude all property with unique historical or natural characteristics, such as historical monuments and most of the national park system. The purpose of a rental charge system is to improve allocation decisions on *marginal* federal uses of real property, and for this purpose it would be sufficient to establish annual rents on only that property that might conceivably be transferred or disposed for other uses.

Annual rents should preferably be established to reflect the highest value of real property in alternative federal *and* nonfederal uses. This rule would create some problems for property whose most valuable alternative use is outside the federal government, because the public land laws restrict the disposal of federal real property. Nevertheless, it would probably be desirable to assess federal real property in terms of its highest value in any alternative use in order to force a recognition of the total cost of maintaining this property in federal use. For much general purpose real property, such as office buildings, the value in alternative federal uses might be sufficiently close to its highest value in any use to make the assessments on this basis.

The obvious organization to perform a traditional assessment role is the General Services Administration. If GSA should be selected for this purpose, some procedure would have to be established to adjudicate any disputes about the assessments that might arise, say, between GSA and the using agency or between GSA and a potential alternative user. A different approach worth serious consideration would be self-assessment by the property-using agencies. This approach would permit each agency to assess all the eligible real property that it used—on the condition, a critical one, that it would be willing to dispose of each unit of property at this assessed value. Such a self-assessment system, which deserves consideration for nonfederal property as well, would be self-policing and would not require any additional procedures for adjudicating disputes or assessments.

The suggested procedure for incorporating annual real property rents into agency budgets would be to add these rents to the outlay ceilings that OMB establishes and against which agencies prepare their proposed budgets. Agencies would be authorized to exceed the ceiling if the sum of budget outlays and rents on real property were within the ceiling on total annual costs. Any real property disposed of by an agency would be maintained by GSA pending transfer to another agency or disposal to a nonfederal user. Thus, under the proposal, the budget concept used in the agency and presidential budget review would be a total annual cost budget, although no change would be made in the scope of the budget reviewed by Congress. By reducing new real property acquisitions and by providing potential offsetting receipts from the sale or outlease of real property, the rental charge system should lead to a reduction in unified budget outlays. For this reason, it should serve the interest of the presidential budget director, although the budget process would be somewhat more complex.

The federal Property Review Board is now considering a proposed rental charge system similar to the one outlined here.[6] Given the magnitude of real property owned by the federal government, these and other alternatives deserve the most careful formulation and evaluation.

**2. Manpower.** As described above, the underfunding of civil service pensions and the unfunding of military pensions are the major conditions that cause the federal budget to understate the total annual cost of current employees. The case for full funding of government pensions is somewhat different from the case for full funding of private pensions: For the federal government, the sole reason for full funding of pensions is to ensure that agencies face up to the total annual cost of current employees. In contrast with a private pension fund, the financial integrity of a federal government pension fund does not require full funding; the government's ability to pay future pension benefits is a function of its future ability to tax, borrow, and print money, and these powers are independent of the accounting commitment of government bonds against the liabilities of a pension fund. If, as is sometimes alleged, federal agency use of manpower is independent of budgeted costs, then there would be no case for full funding of federal pensions. Federal agencies, however, probably respond to changes in factor costs much like all other organizations, and a differential increase in manpower costs due to full funding of pensions would surely lead them to more efficient use of manpower.

The underfunding of civil service pensions could be most easily corrected by doubling the present agency contributions per employee. This would leave the net income of employees constant but would increase the cost of civil service manpower to the agencies by 7 percent. The objective of this increase would be served only if the increased pension funding were included in agency budgets and not by some manipulation of the pension accounts. In order to implement this increase, the Office of Management and Budget should add 7 percent of civil service manpower costs to the budget outlay ceilings for each agency. This reform should reduce total annual costs, but it

[6] The initial OMB response to this rental charge proposal was strongly negative. This response, primarily reflecting the views of the management staff, included the following general conclusions: (1) OMB requirements that agencies report any "excess" property are sufficient to assure effective property management; (2) the combination of resources used by agencies would not be significantly changed by changing the budgeted costs of these resources; (3) federal payments to state and local governments should not be a function of federal real property in these areas. This reaction, to be blunt, does not reflect the general quality of OMB analysis.

is not clear that it would reduce current budget outlays and, thus, serve the interests of the budget director.

Full funding of military pensions could be achieved without establishing a formal pension fund, as the accounting commitment of government bonds against pension liabilities serves no obvious purpose. The desired effect could be achieved by modifying the fiscal guidance to the military services and defense agencies as follows: (1) Delete the payments to currently retired military personnel from the fiscal guidance to each service and, preferably also but less important, from the Department of Defense budget. These payments reflect prior use of military manpower and are independent of current military forces and manpower policies. (2) Add an estimate of the increase in pension liabilities attributable to current military manpower to the fiscal guidance to each service and defense agency. These estimates, which will be a function of the grade structure and retirement patterns of each service and expected future salary increases, should probably be prepared in the Office of the Secretary of Defense and checked by the Office of Management and Budget. Under these two changes, the average cost of current military manpower, as reflected in the service budgets subject to review at the departmental and presidential level, would increase by 15 to 20 percent but with very wide variations among military personnel. On net, the military services should support this reform because the budget outlays for retired personnel are now higher than the increase in pension liabilities and this difference will increase rapidly in the next decade. Again, this reform should reduce total annual costs, but it is not clear whether it would also reduce current budget outlays.

The other conditions that cause budget outlays for military manpower to understate total annual cost are now both less important and more difficult to change without the understanding and approval of Congress. A case can be made for eliminating all or most prospective veterans benefits for those who enter the military after the termination of conscription. (The one type of benefit that should probably be maintained is medical care and compensation for service-connected disabilities, given the difficulty of insuring against these disabilities.) This reform would place the total cost of current military manpower in the DOD budget, rather than in some future Veterans Administration budget. If it is to be initiated, the opportune time would be when the country shifts to an all-volunteer army in mid-1973. This timing would deter the military services from using veterans benefits as recruiting aids and would make it clear that the shift was the basis for this reform. The value of this reform, unfortunately, is unlikely to be appreciated by the budget director because it might increase budget outlays in the short term as the price of substantially reducing outlays in the more distant future. As a rule and for understandable reasons, it is difficult to convince budget directors of the merit of such reforms, at least in the absence of external guidance. For example, termination of conscription had to be initiated and supported outside the agencies and the budget office because, however desirable, it increased budget outlays for the same amount of military personnel.

**3. Nuclear materials.** Annual cost budgeting of nuclear materials and weapons can also be achieved by changes in the fiscal guidance process without changing the nature of the budget subject to congressional review. The first step would be to delete the cost of defense-related AEC activities from the fiscal guidance to the AEC and to add these annual costs to the fiscal guidance to the Department of Defense. The Office of Management and Budget should probably be responsible for making the estimate of the cost of defense-related AEC activities, since AEC would have an obvious incentive to underestimate these costs. AEC, thus, would be asked to prepare a budget only for its civilian activities within a budget ceiling restricted to these activities. The Department of Defense, in contrast, would be asked to prepare a budget to include the cost of its own activities, plus the cost of those materials and services it demands from the AEC.[7] For this system to be effective, the presidential budget director would have to be willing to approve a higher budget for the Department of Defense if the defense demands on AEC are reduced. The Office of Management and Budget of the National Security Council would have to initiate this reform, because neither DOD nor the AEC has the correct incentive.

At this time, more study is needed to determine whether the Department of Defense should be charged a rent on the existing stock of nuclear materials. A careful estimate of the total and annual value of these materials should be made, given the estimated demand for reactor fuel and the rate of releasing the nonweapons inventory. If the annual value of this stock of material is much less than $1 billion, the establishment of a rental charge system might not be worthwhile. Charging Defense only for new materials would be sufficient to achieve an efficient allocation if any new materials are demanded at full marginal cost. A rental charge system, if estab-

[7] A similar proposal was made recently by the House Appropriations Committee. See House Report 92-1389, pp. 35-36.

lished, should have the following general characteristics: annual rents on nuclear material should be estimated in terms of the current value of this material as commercial reactor fuel. The total rent on the existing stock of material should be added to the fiscal guidance to the Department of Defense, and, in turn, to the separate services and defense agencies. Any material released by DOD would be returned to the AEC, either for blending down into reactor fuel or for new weapons.

Again, this system would be effective only if the budget director were willing to approve higher budget outlays for DOD if its actions reduce total annual cost. In this case, however, any material released by DOD either reduces AEC budget outlays or provides offsetting receipts from the sale of nuclear materials. Successful development of a "breeder" reactor (which produces more fuel than it consumes), of course, would sharply reduce the value of the existing stock of nuclear materials and, thus, also reduce the value of any rental charge system designed to improve the allocation of these materials.

**4. Nonmarketed resources.** More study is needed of the two major nonmarketed resources, the electronic frequency spectrum and the airspace and air traffic control services, in order to be able to estimate the value of these resources and to evaluate alternative allocation mechanisms. Some current efforts should provide a better understanding of the allocation of these resources. The Office of Telecommunications Policy is conducting an internal study of alternative mechanisms for allocating that part of the spectrum now used by the federal government, and this effort is expected to lead to more detailed studies. Ultimately, the frequency spectrum will be better managed only when some market for spectrum rights is developed, and this will require legislation and a change in the role of the Federal Communications Commission. In addition, the Federal Aviation Agency will soon publish a study of the allocation of the costs of the air traffic control system among the major user classes, and this study could provide the basis for establishing a system of user fees based on the marginal public outlays of supplying air traffic control services. Efficient management of the airspace and the air traffic control system probably will require a system of en route and terminal fees, both to ration the congested airspace and to finance the desired air traffic control services.[8]

[8] Ross Eckert, *Airports and Congestion: A Problem of Misplaced Subsidies* (Washington, D. C.: American Enterprise Institute, 1972), makes a good case for restructuring the general system of landing fees.

## Summary Comments

Each of the above problems has been recognized for many years, as has the general character of the proposed solutions. With the exception of the termination of military manpower conscription, however, little progress has been made to resolve these problems. Since the federal agencies usually do not have the right incentives for resolving these problems, the initiative must come from the office of the President or, possibly, from Congress. Given the difficulty of developing the necessary institutional solutions, consideration should be given to setting up separate study groups for each of these resources, and charging them with the task of creating the appropriate budgeting and allocation mechanisms by a specified deadline. This chapter has argued that this type of serious, sustained attention to major unbudgeted costs will be necessary to achieve an efficient use of these resources.

# 3
# FUTURE COSTS

## The Problem

For some years, even prior to the development of the formal Planning, Programming, and Budgeting System, the Bureau of the Budget and selected federal agencies routinely estimated and presented the future budget costs of present decisions. Such information was generally available in detail to the agency and presidential budget reviews and, in a more summary form, to the congressional budget review. However, the availability of these estimates did not, by itself, create a willingness to use them to control future costs, and for the most part, these estimates were ignored. Recognition that these estimates seldom affected current decisions led to deterioration in the quality and availability of the estimates, while concern that the budget review *ought* to pay attention to future costs led to periodic attempts to develop and present the estimates. The requirement of the Legislative Reorganization Act of 1970 to the effect that estimates of the five-year costs for all federal programs requiring new authorizing legislation be prepared and presented to Congress is only the latest manifestation of concern about future costs. But this act did not mandate the necessary changes in the budget process to make these estimates more relevant to current decisions.

This cycle will probably be repeated unless the budget process is changed to institutionalize a concern about future costs. The mere presentation of data on the future costs of present decisions has much the same effect as the presentation of data on the external costs of any activity—some waste motion, an ephemeral sense of guilt, but little impact on the spending stream. (The same general observation would also apply to program evaluation activities.) The problems generated by these external costs will not be resolved until the decision processes are changed to internalize these costs.

The future costs of present government decisions are largely external to the decision process as a consequence of the following conditions:

- The annual budget cycle requires decisions on present budget authority, and any estimates of future costs constitute only supplementary information about which no decisions must be made.
- The Constitution limits the power of one Congress to bind the spending decisions of the successor Congress, and this restricts the ability of the executive branch to achieve a desired multi-year budget path.
- The median tenure of budget directors and members of the cabinet is around two years. This limited tenure, combined with the condition cited next, minimizes the concern about the future costs and problems of present decisions.
- Most important, in government there is no analogue to the corporate "stock option" that could be used to induce present officials to be concerned about the "net worth" of government institutions at the end of their tenure. An official's concern about his reputation may serve this purpose but does not appear sufficiently strong to overcome the understandable incentive to defer costs and problems.

Under these conditions, a problem deferred can become a problem avoided. Moreover, these conditions provide the necessary opening for the "foot-in-the-door" budget technique: gain approval for a program that calls for small current spending but implies a commitment to large future spending. These conditions also weaken the incentive to reduce spending. For several large federal programs, a major reduction in current budget authority would yield little current reduction in spending, because most current spending derives from prior budget authority. A presidential budget director would have to be a saint to bear the blame for reducing a program like urban renewal or federal housing that would lead to reduced outlays only after several years; for all their obvious qualifications, budget directors are not noted for this characteristic. In sum, these conditions lead to near indifference about the future costs of present decisions and are largely responsible for the uncontrollability, from the perspective of the presidential budget review, of over two-thirds of federal budget outlays. Any plan that seeks to institutionalize concern about future costs would necessarily entail measures for changing or offsetting the above conditions.

## A Suggested Structural Reform

The four conditions summarized above severely limit the proposal to institutionalize concern about future costs. The reform discussed in this chapter accepts these conditions as given and focuses on changes in the budget process within the executive branch designed to offset the problems created by these conditions. These reforms would not require the understanding and approval of Congress but, at some future time, some changes in the congressional budget review process may also be desirable.

The suggested reforms would create a multi-year budget process within the executive branch, possibly starting with the fiscal 1975 budget cycle. They are offered with some reservations, because they would substantially complicate the budget process and would not foreclose the opportunities for the agencies and Congress to "game" the process. The process would involve the following steps:

1. As part of the spring reviews conducted by the Office of Management and Budget, outlay estimates would be prepared for all present programs, for all new programs expected to be approved in the new fiscal year, and for all changes proposed by the executive office for the first planning year. The estimates would be made for the planning year and *four* subsequent fiscal years. This step represents only a minor change from the present spring review process, and many of these estimates are now required by the Legislative Reorganization Act of 1970.

2. As part of the present budget process, just following the spring reviews, OMB establishes outlay ceilings for the major agencies for the planning year. The first major change to a multi-year budget process would be to establish agency budget ceilings in terms of the *discounted sum* of agency outlays for the planning year and the four subsequent fiscal years. The planning ceiling, thus, would be a five-year outlay ceiling with earlier years weighted more than later years in this period. The discount rate in any year would be the same for all agencies. Two alternative criteria should be considered in selecting a discount rate:

(1) The discount rate for each year could be used as a fiscal instrument to reflect the expected relative tightness of the federal budget in each year. For example, the rate would be higher in very tight budget years and lower in years for which a surplus is expected.

(2) The most appropriate discount rate is probably the nearly constant opportunity cost of federal spending—that is, the

average rate of return, before taxes and after inflation, on all investments in the nonfederal sector. This rate is around 10 percent a year. Use of this rate would constrain federal spending for projects that do not yield a corresponding return and, thus, would contribute to an efficient allocation of resources between federal and nonfederal activities.

3. Agencies would then prepare their proposed budgets subject to the five-year discounted outlay ceilings. Agencies would have the opportunity to propose any pattern of outlays over the five years, subject to the ceiling on the discounted sum of outlays. This procedure presents the agencies with an interesting tradeoff: on the one hand, they could spend more in early years if they reduced their outlays in later years. This would make it easier to finance highly productive capital investments that are often difficult to fit into a one-year budget ceiling. On the other hand, agencies could increase their total spending by reducing spending in the early years, because early spending is weighted more in the discounting calculation. Agencies have a general incentive to spend more in the early years and this incentive would tend to prevent their gaming the process by proposing that the total discounted outlays be spent in the later years. They might still try the opposite tactic of proposing that total discounted outlays be spent in the early years, counting on continued support for the program's purposes and benefits to ensure additional funding in the later years. Any type of rule, of course, is subject to some gaming. However, knowledge of an agency's incentives, combined with periodic review and willingness to impose some sanctions, is usually sufficient to deter the grossest abuses.

Under the plan, the agency budgets submitted to OMB in the early fall would present the agency's proposed outlays for each year in the five-year period. This step, a major change from the present process, is designed to force agencies to recognize the future costs of present decisions and to induce them to consider shifting outlays among years in a manner consistent with the general fiscal objectives of the President.

4. The OMB fall budget review would determine the presidential proposal for program and agency outlays for each of the five years. Only the proposed budgets for the first planning year would be presented to Congress. The agencies would be informed, however, of the program and agency outlay levels approved for the four subsequent years, and these future budgets would represent a present administration commitment to support these budget levels in the

absence of substantially changed conditions. This process would be effective only to the extent the agencies were assured of a presidential commitment to support these future outlay levels—subject, of course, to the continuation of the administration.

One issue that must be resolved concerns the nature of the dollars in which the future outlay commitments would be expressed. Should the administration's commitment to a future outlay level be expressed in terms of (1) the specific prices faced by the agency, (2) the general prices faced by the government, (3) the general price level in the private sector, or (4) nominal dollars? Use of the specific prices facing each agency would roughly maintain the approved purchasing power of each program but would eliminate any agency incentives to increase productivity or resist specific price increases. Use of the general price level faced by the government would somewhat change the purchasing power among programs and would strengthen the agencies' incentives to resist specific price increases, but would reduce their incentives to resist price increases (such as civil service salaries) that would affect all agencies. (The British experiment with a similar multi-year budget process uses this alternative, but not without problems.) [1] The appropriate resolution of this issue would be to express the outlay commitment in terms of the general price level in the private sector. This alternative would somewhat change the allocation of real resources among agencies and to the government, but would strengthen the incentives of the agencies, individually and collectively, to increase productivity and to resist price increases facing the government. Finally, use of nominal dollars would be the simplest to administer and would strengthen the agencies' incentives to resist a general price inflation. For this reason, some British Treasury officials favor this alternative. On the other hand, the general price level is most directly responsive to actions by the monetary authorities, and there seems to be little purpose served in penalizing the spending agencies for general inflation. The above considerations suggest that some general index of prices in the private sector, such as the consumer expenditure deflator, should be used to modify the approved future year outlays.

5. Total federal outlays for each of the five years would be determined by summing the approved program and agency budgets. The budget director would be charged with demonstrating to the President that total outlays in *each* of the five years were consistent with accepted fiscal policy, whatever that policy might be. This step

---

[1] See Wildavsky, *Community and Policy,* for a summary of the British experience with a similar multi-year budget process, the Public Expenditure Survey System.

would constrain the budget director from meeting the fiscal target in the first planning year only by deferring outlays that, in total, exceeded the fiscal targets for the subsequent years. It would probably also be desirable for the President's budget as presented to Congress to set forth the proposed total outlays for each of the five years, for this would demonstrate a prior commitment to maintaining the selected fiscal policy throughout the five-year period. It should be recognized that this procedure would eliminate one of the major short-term devices a budget director uses to meet a fiscal target—in order to discourage him from deferring problems to later years. A budget director with a short expected tenure would probably object to this reform on the ground (that deserves sympathy) that he has too little control of the budget in the short run. The President and members of Congress, however, have a longer tenure, so any initiative for a multi-year budget process is probably dependent on their concern about the longer range budget outlook.

6. In the next budget cycle, the approved outlay levels for the four later years plus a new estimate for the fifth year would provide the basis for developing a new multi-year budget. The earlier approved outlay levels would be changed only if there were a demonstrated change in conditions (such as inflation or unexpected changes in beneficiary populations, et cetera), new congressional actions, or a change in the administration's objectives. The process would then proceed by the same steps as in the prior cycle.

**Summary Comments**

Whatever the merits of annual review of the federal budget (and a case could be made for a longer cycle or continuous review), it is important to recognize that a one-year cycle is deeply ingrained in the political traditions and processes of the federal government. The distinguishing characteristic of the multi-year budget process suggested here is that *it would develop an annual proposed budget as part of a five-year budget review within the executive branch.* Both the one-year review cycle and the five-year budget planning period are somewhat arbitrary. Maybe a two-year review cycle and a four-year planning period would harmonize better with the "rhythm" of federal election cycles. In any case, a five-year planning period has some precedent in the defense planning process and in the information requirements of the Legislative Reorganization Act of 1970. The five-year period suggested is only illustrative and is not the only period consistent with the suggested multi-year budget process. As summarized above, the suggested reform does not require the approval of Congress, but experience with a multi-year budget process might lead Congress to review its own budget process.

For several years, the British government has used a "rolling" five-year budget process that is similar to the one outlined above.[2] In Great Britain, of course, the budget review process is somewhat less complex than ours because the cabinet is a select committee of the parliamentary majority. The administrative mechanics of the British system have proved to be manageable but complicated. On the other hand, experience under it suggests that a multi-year budget process, by itself, should not be expected to resolve the fundamental problems of achieving a political consensus or of controlling the bureaucracy; and at this time, it is difficult to discern any significant improvement in the quality of Britain's budget decisions. One predictable problem the British experiment has faced is that the agencies regard the approved future budgets as floors on future spending (rather than ceilings) and as bases for bargaining increases with the government. This response is similar to the response of U.S. federal agencies to the annual budget "ceilings" established by the Office of Management and Budget. This suggests that the effectiveness of any government budget process is dependent on the rewards and sanctions used by political officials to control the bureaucracy.

In summary, this chapter makes a case for experimenting with a multi-year budget process within the executive branch. This proposal is not offered as a panacea. Further changes would be required to achieve effective political control and efficient budget decisions, and the experiment might prove that the reform was not worth the cost. Because of the magnitude of the future problems created by our present annual budget process, however, serious consideration of the experiment is merited.

---

[2] Ibid.

# 4
# POLICY FORMULATION

## The Problem

The time has long passed, if there was ever such a time, when the President was expected to function only as the chief executive of the federal government, leaving policy formulation and review entirely to Congress. Far from being an appointed executive who serves at the will of Congress, the President is the only federal official (along with the Vice President) who is elected by a national constituency. The importance of his role in initiating proposed changes in federal policy is probably derived more from this fact than from the increasing size and complexity of the government. In the early years of this century, Congress itself recognized the policy initiation role of the President by establishing the executive budget and by requesting the President's proposals for policy changes.

After more than 50 years of experience with the executive budget process, however, the Executive Office of the President has yet to organize an effective policy formulation and review process. The present process of formulating the President's policy proposals entails several major flaws.[1]

1. In attempting to develop a coherent budget policy review process that serves the interest of the President, the Office of Management and Budget receives very little explicit prior policy guidance. As a rule, OMB's staff and, apparently, most of its leadership must *infer* policy guidance on desirable and feasible actions from prior decisions on related actions and from prior public statements by the

[1] Most of the observations in this section are necessarily from my own experience. Unfortunately, a good study of OMB and the other major units of the executive office has yet to be written.

President. Neither prior decisions nor public statements, however, provide a very explicit guidance on current issues. A prior decision may have reflected the administration's preferences in conditions that have since changed, may have been an action that the administration viewed as the least unfavorable of the then probable alternatives, or may have been an action that the administration did not favor except in exchange for support of some other preferred action; in none of these cases can a prior decision provide effective guidance on a current issue. Public statements present the same type of problem. They are a *rationalization* of decisions made for a complex set of reasons, and cannot provide the *rationale* for future decisions. The effect is that a conscientious member of the OMB staff is usually operating in the dark, without any clear perception of the administration's objectives or its view of the political constraints or feasible actions. This condition is also characteristic of other presidential offices, departmental staffs, and agency staffs.

A perceived absence of guidance may be due to any one or more of three conditions. It may occur because the President and his associates do not know what they want to achieve in a specific area. Or it may be that they choose not to convey their views (or the lack thereof) to the relevant staffs, possibly to avoid premature disclosure or a public debate on the guidance. Or possibly the guidance process is too "noisy" for the intended signals to be perceived by the staffs. As a rule, the OMB staff cannot distinguish among these conditions. All it can perceive is that guidance, if it exists, is not getting through.

In the absence of politics, it is sometimes suggested, OMB could put out a good budget. This attitude avoids the main issue, however, because political officials will evaluate the effectiveness of the budget process by political measures. The problem is not to divorce budget making from politics, but to make the proposed budget a more effective instrument of the political interests of the President. The political process may not always serve the public interest, but that problem must be resolved by changing the political process, not the budget process.

2. OMB, and the executive office in general, does not have a formal process of policy formulation and review. For the most part, policy decisions are made by default, in a hurried and ad hoc response to proposals originating elsewhere. Three conditions characterize the present policy review process:

First, the executive office review processes are generally captive of history, of present programs and policies. Only rarely do they address the following types of questions:

• If there were no policy or program in a specific area, what policy or program would be desirable?

• What is the basis for federal action, in terms of the Constitution, the efficient division of roles between private and public activities, and the efficient division of roles between the federal and state-local governments?

• How should a new policy or program be managed in terms of the objectives against which the program and managers would be evaluated, the incentives of the managing agencies, the division of responsibility within the bureaucracy, and the nature of the performance review process?

• What is the optimal strategy for moving from present programs and policies to those desired, in terms of packaging the proposal for the public and Congress, bringing the bureaucracy along, countering other probable centers of opposition, and possibly providing indemnity for private losers?

Some of these questions are addressed at later stages in the review process, but often only by Congress, and sometimes only after new legislation defines the general policy outline. The President, as well as the public, however, is not well served by a failure to address such questions concerning existing programs or prior to proposing new policies and programs.

Second, the executive office review processes are primarily responsive to proposals made by the agencies, by Congress, by the opposition party, and by special interest groups. Only rarely does the Executive Office of the President initiate a proposal of its own and organize the effort to gain approval for the proposal. Moreover, only rarely does OMB develop a credible alternative to proposals made by others. Instead, its usual response is to approve the proposal at a slightly lower level of near-term funding or to deny it.

Third, the OMB review processes, in particular, are too objective. In an adversary proceeding, if one party is an advocate and the other party is objective, the advocate usually wins. The OMB review processes, in effect, constitute a budget "court," but one without any developed case for spending much less or spending nothing. If OMB does not forcefully advocate spending less, the President loses power over the agencies (because he will have nothing to give back to them on appeal) and Congress becomes the only effective budgetmaker. The Office of Management and Budget is regarded by many people in the agencies, in Congress, and among the public as a very powerful organization, even though federal spending has been increasing at a rapid rate. A possibly more accurate characterization is that OMB is the referee, scorekeeper, and broadcaster of the presidential budget review process and not a significant contributor to presidential budget policy. Maybe Congress and the President expect no more of OMB. The size of the federal budget and the general sense of a budget crisis, however, probably demand a more assertive role—one that would be approved by both Congress and the President.

## A Suggested Structural Reform

The suggested changes in the presidential policy guidance and review process would require action only within the executive office. This reform is designed to strengthen the President's control of this process—and, of course, to improve the quality of the output of this process. Nevertheless, many members of Congress would probably support this reform, as Congress now wastes considerable time reviewing poorly conceived and formulated presidential proposals. This problem is not specific to the present administration but derives from the role of the President's budget in presenting many, and maybe most, proposals for major changes in policy. This problem would not exist, of course, if Congress had the sole policy formulation role, but as stated earlier, a major policy initiating role for the President appears to be an accepted characteristic of the federal political process.

It is important to recognize that some guidance to the presidential staffs would be better than none, even if it should lead to waste motion or have to be corrected later. At the present time, the costs of redundant staff work on major federal policies and programs would be far less than the costs of inadequate staff work. A greater sense of direction and movement is necessary in order to maintain the discipline, coordination, and morale of the presidential staffs.

The first challenge is to institutionalize a political guidance process within the executive office. Some executive office unit, probably the Domestic Council staff, should be charged with preparing a set of guidance papers on major concerns of administration. If prior guidance is still effective, it should be repeated. If prior guidance had not been understood, it should be clarified. Generally, these guidance papers should be available prior to the OMB spring reviews, and these reviews could be used to clarify the guidance. These reviews, thus, would have a function similar to that of the hearings on authorizing legislation in Congress, leaving to the fall budget reviews a role similar to that of the appropriations hearings. Such a two-step process within Congress has had obvious problems but has proved its value over a long period.

In any year, the major focus of the guidance papers and the OMB spring reviews would be those major programs due for new authorizing legislation in the next cycle, programs on which major public debate is expected, and programs where the administration expects to propose a significant change in policy. New policy guidance papers, thus, should be written on every major program once every several years. But, in any one year, the guidance papers and the spring reviews would focus on only those federal programs that most demand current attention. After the spring reviews, the guidance would be reformulated in agency dimensions and transmitted to the agencies with their budget ceilings. These memoranda to the agencies would both describe the general characteristics of the administration's objectives for specific programs and the outlay ceiling (or discounted five-year outlay ceiling, as described in Chapter 3) against which their budgets should be planned. Some effort would be necessary to develop a formal guidance process, with the Domestic Council having the primary role, but an experiment appears worthwhile.

The second challenge is to establish a formal policy review process within the executive office. The obvious way to meet this challenge is to continue to develop the OMB spring reviews in the direction initiated in 1971 and 1972. In these years, the instructions for the spring reviews focused attention on the major questions (summarized above) that must be addressed in an effective policy review. But only a few sessions actually followed this model. In general, too many issues were addressed that did not need OMB leadership attention at that time, the range of alternatives considered was unnecessarily restricted by prior judgments of political feasibility, there was insufficient attention to potential program reductions and terminations, and these reviews were conducted without any more than the most general guidance as to the objectives and concerns of the President. In addition, there should be a more direct relation between the spring reviews and the focus and timing of major studies in order to ensure that the appropriate background studies are performed and thereby to improve the quality of subsequent reviews. In general, however, the OMB spring reviews are developing in a productive direction and appear to be the best forum for an effective policy review. As the OMB division that organized these reviews has been disbanded, some other OMB units should be given the explicit institutional responsibility for organizing both these reviews and the flow of studies contributing to them.

## Summary Comments

The suggested changes in the policy guidance and review process within the executive branch are based on a recognition that the federal policy formulation role is shared by both the President and Congress. The objective of these suggestions is not to strengthen the President relative to Congress, but to improve the quality of the final policy decisions. In the final analysis, if Congress is responding to better formulated proposals from the executive branch, its constitutional role in reviewing and approving major policy changes will be strengthened. The "proof is in the pudding." Our present processes are not serving us well, and some experiment with the type of policy guidance and review process within the executive branch that is suggested here deserves serious consideration.

Book and cover design: Pat Taylor